I0792793

Leonardo Dreams of His Flying Machine

Charles Anthony Silvestri - Anne Horjus

ACROTERION BOOKS

For Emma, about to take her giant leap.
C.A.S.

For Sjoukje
A.H.

Poem copyright ©2001 by Charles Anthony Silvestri
Appendix text copyright ©2020 by Charles Anthony Silvestri and Anne Horjus
Illustrations copyright ©2020 by Anne Horjus

The poem "Leonardo Dreams of His Flying Machine" was first published in 2001 by Walton Music Publishing. It also appears in *A Silver Thread*: *The Lyric Poetry of Charles Anthony Silvestri* (G.I.A. 2018).

All rights reserved. For information about permission to reproduce sections of this book, write to Acroterion Books, 5305 Harvard Road, Lawrence, KS 66049-48781.

www.acroterionbooks.com

This book was printed by Worzalla Press in Stevens Point, WI
The text in this book is set in Cochin and Minion Pro
The illustrations were created using oil on birch panel; silverpoint on prepared paper; pen-and-ink, charcoal, and red chalk on paper; and digital media.

Silvestri, Charles Anthony
Leonardo Dreams of His Flying Machine / written by Charles Anthony Silvestri ; illustrated by Anne Horjus
p. cm.
Summary: Leonardo Da Vinci imagines flight, a dream taken up by others who succeed where he failed.
EAN/ISBN-13: 978-1-5400-6880-4
Library of Congress Control Number: 2019919198
[1. Leonardo Da Vinci-Inventor. 2. American Poetry]

Manufactured in the United States of America
1 3 5 7 9 10 8 6 4 2

Exclusively Distributed By
Hal•Leonard® Corporation
7777 W. Bluemound Rd. P.O. Box 13819 Milwaukee, WI 53213

Leonardo Dreams of His Flying Machine

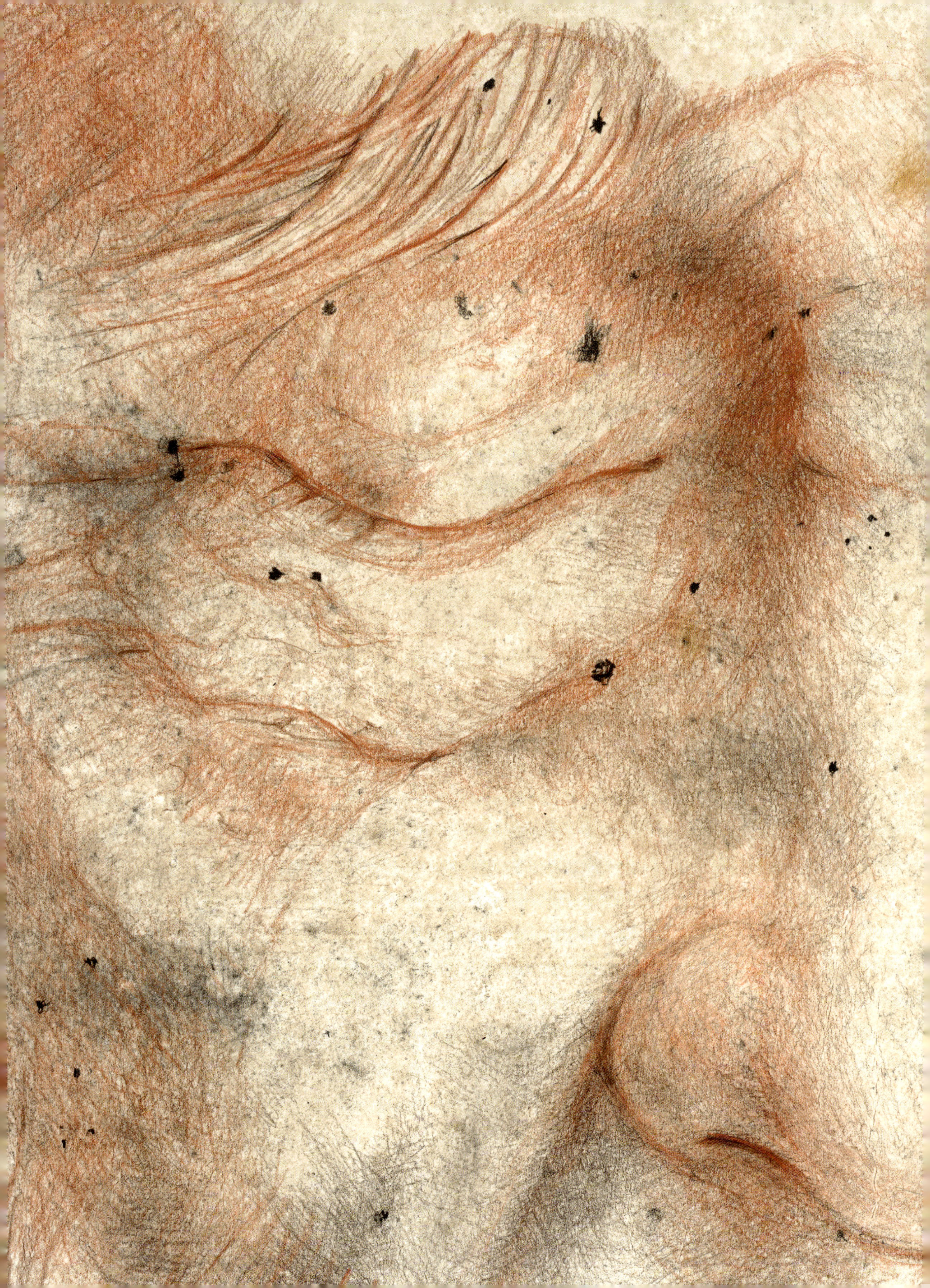

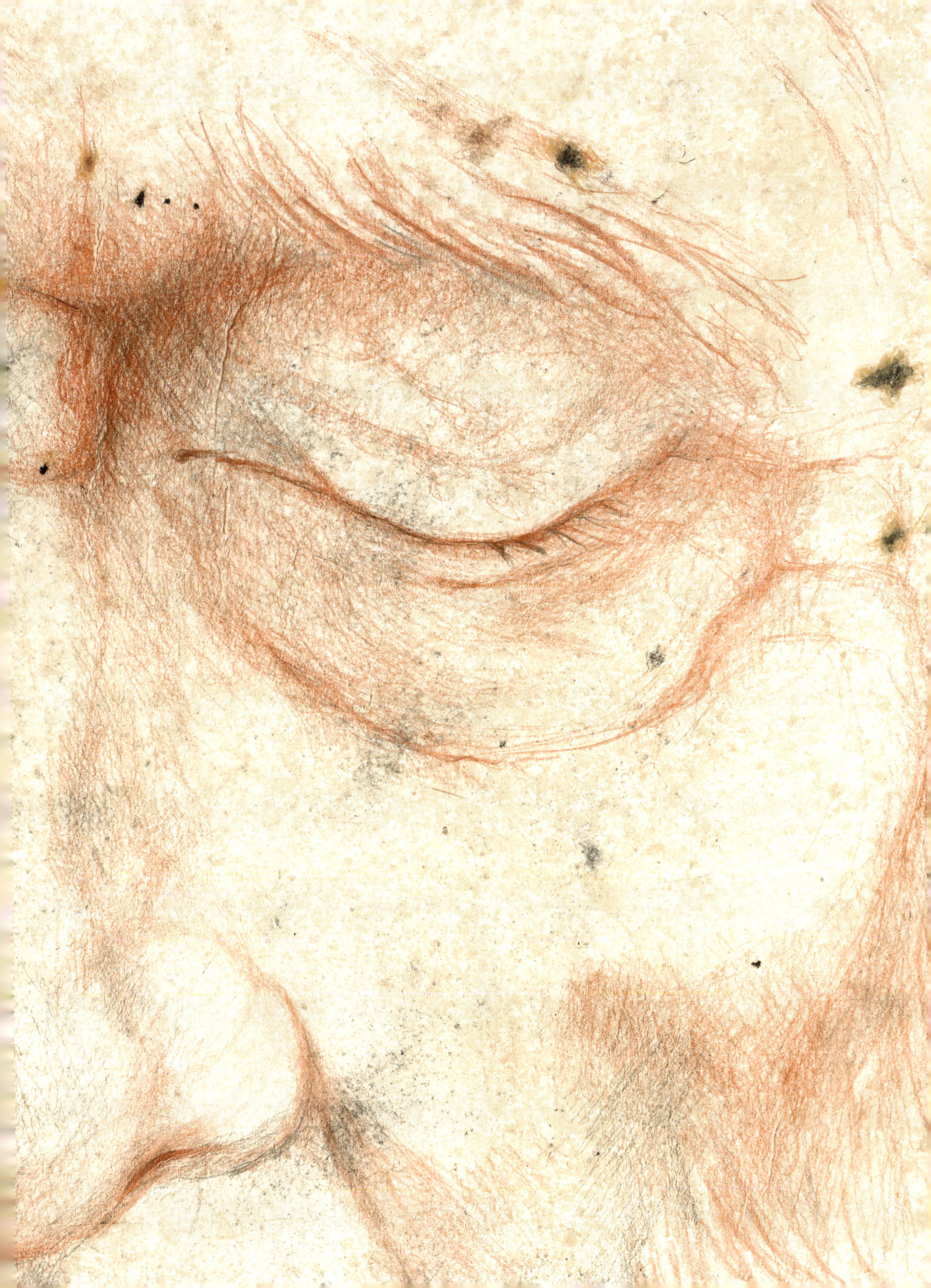

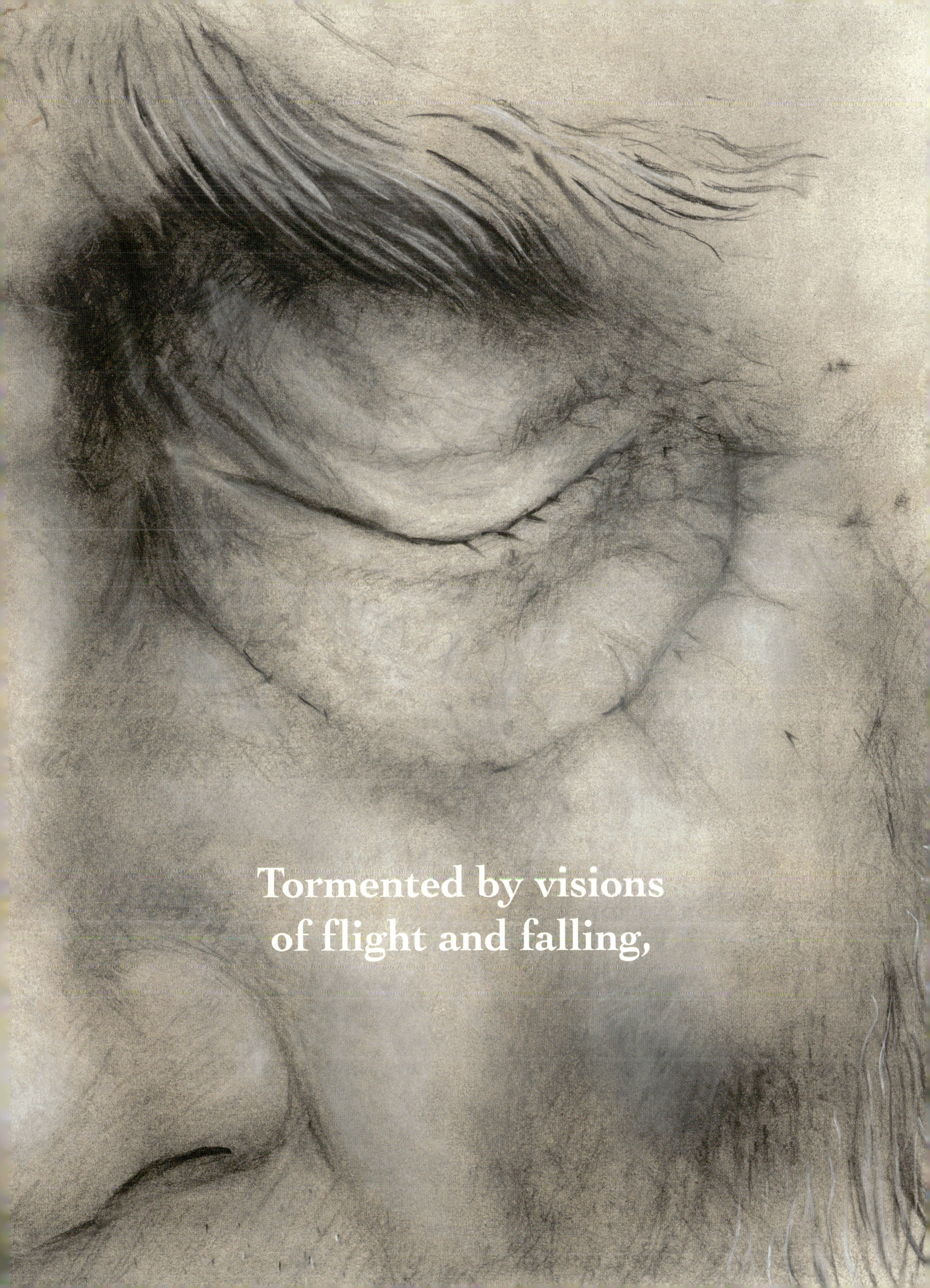

Tormented by visions
of flight and falling,

More wondrous and terrible
each than the last,

Master Leonardo imagines an engine to carry a man up

into the sun...

And as he's dreaming the heavens call him,
softly whispering their siren-song:

"Leonardo, Leonardo, vieni á volare."
"Leonardo, Leonardo, come fly."

L'uomo colle sua congiegniate e grandi ale, facciendo forza contro alla resistente aria.

A man with wings large enough and duly connected, might learn to overcome the resistance of the air.

As the candles burn low
he paces and writes,
releasing purchased pigeons one by one

into the golden Tuscan sunrise...

And as he dreams, again the calling,
the very air itself gives voice:

"Leonardo, Leonardo, vieni á volare,"
"Leonardo, Leonardo, come fly,"
vicina all'elemento del fuoco...
close to the sphere of elemental fire...

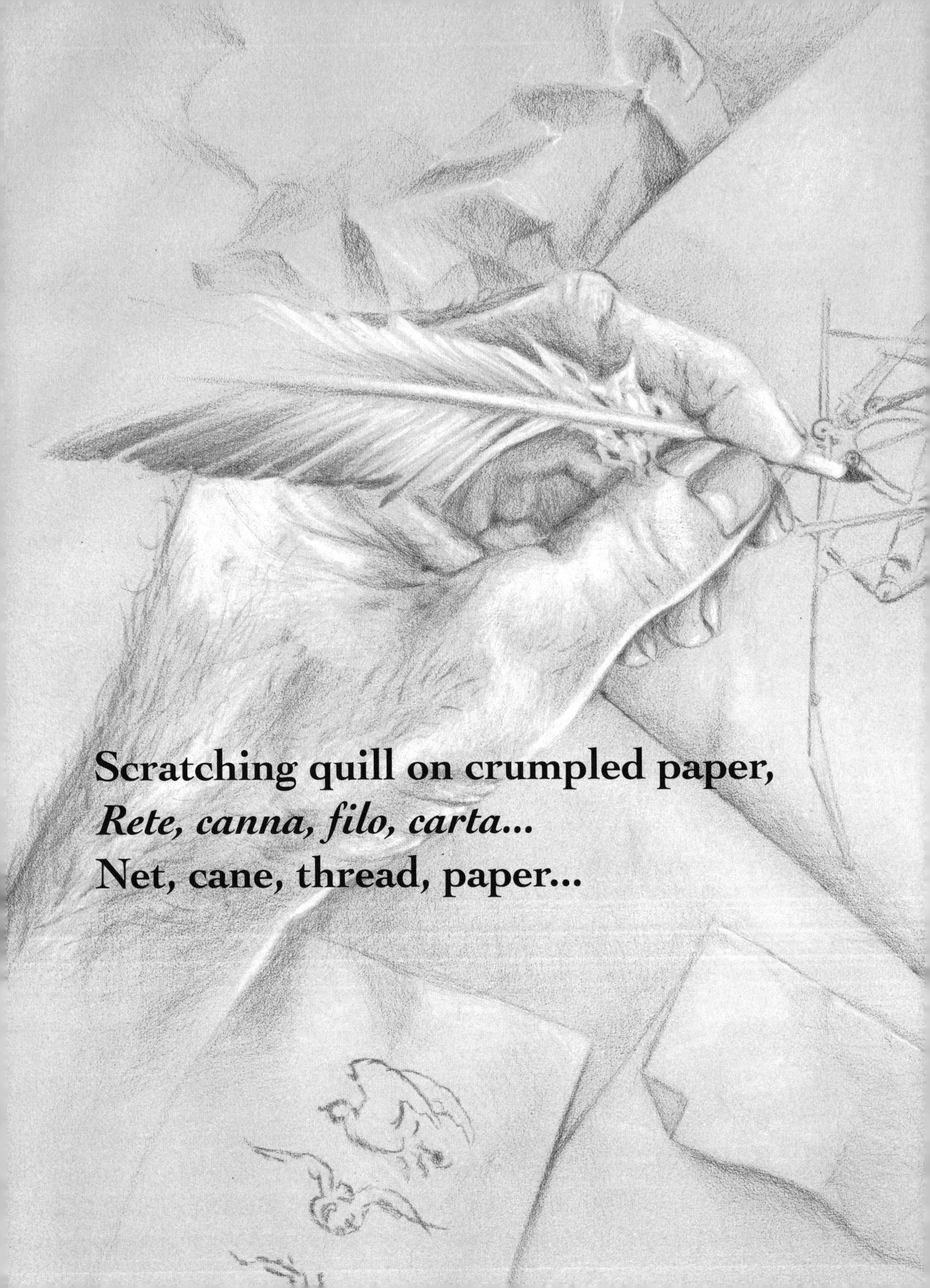

Scratching quill on crumpled paper,
Rete, canna, filo, carta...
Net, cane, thread, paper...

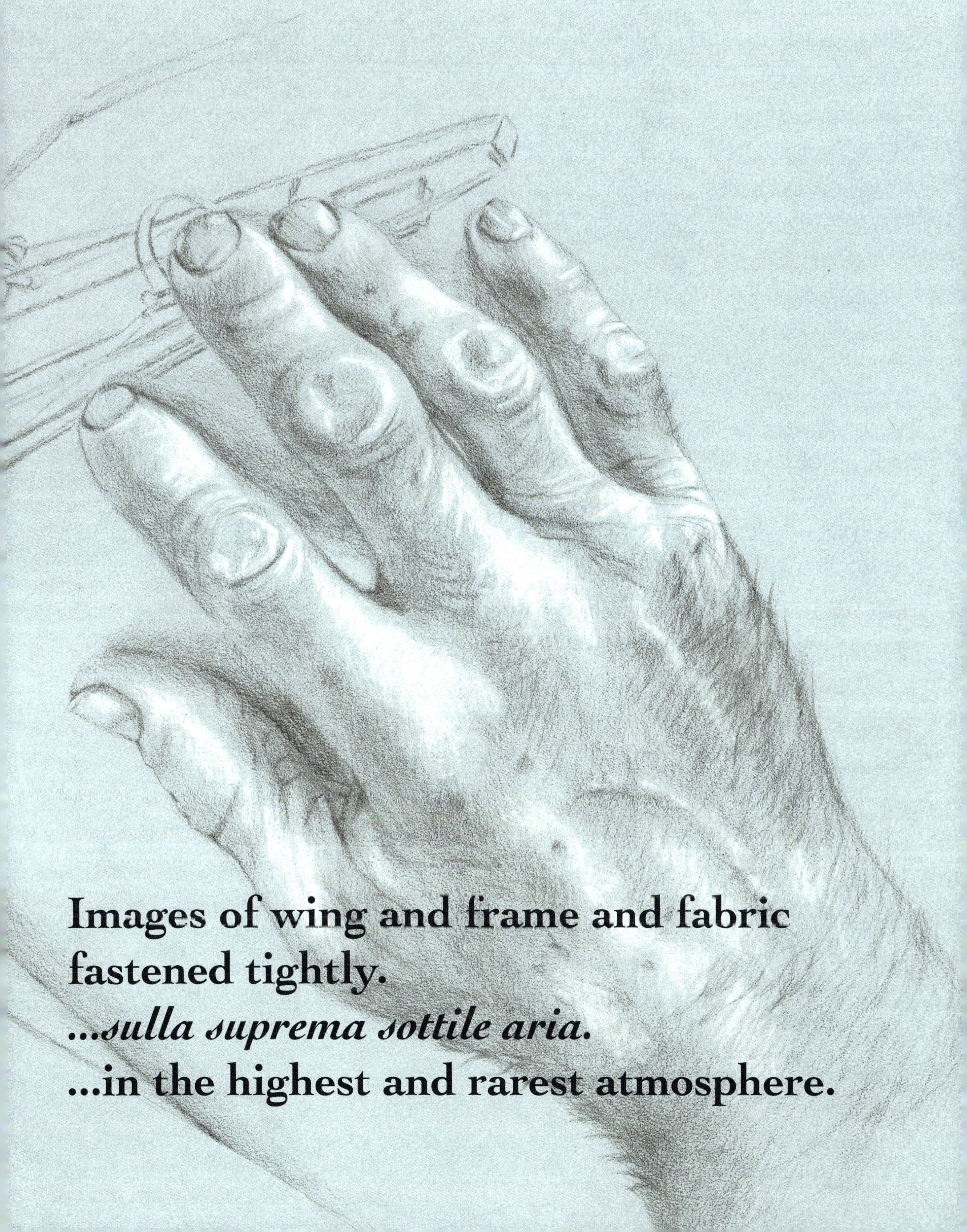

Images of wing and frame and fabric fastened tightly.
...sulla suprema sottile aria.
...in the highest and rarest atmosphere.

As the midnight watchtower tolls,
over rooftop, street and dome,
the triumph of a human being ascending
in the dreaming of a mortal man!

Leonardo steels himself,
takes one last breath,

and leaps...

*"Leonardo, vieni á volare!
Leonardo, sognare!"*

"Leonardo, come fly!
Leonardo, dream!"

Portrait of a Man in Red Chalk - c. 1510

LEONARDO BRIEF BIO

Leonardo di ser Piero da Vinci was born in Vinci, a very small town in central Italy. He was the oldest of many brothers and sisters. When he was fourteen he was made an apprentice to the great Florentine master artist Andrea del Verrocchio. From his master he learned all manner of arts, from painting to sculpture, metal and leather work, carpentry, and so many other useful and wondrous skills. When he was twenty-one he became a Master in his own right, and began his career as an artist. He moved around a lot in his lifetime, mostly in pursuit of noble patrons who would help him fulfill his dream of constructing a grand bronze statue of a horse. Alas, another noble failure... But in his many journeys between Florence, Milan, Rome, and France he learned a great deal, and conversed with many learned and powerful men and women—royalty and peasants alike. These patrons and companions shared his curiosity and imagination, and it was in his work for them that his dreams of flying took shape. Throughout his long life he never lost his curiosity, his desire to create, or to stretch the limits of what human beings could achieve!

LEONARDO AND MUSIC

In addition to his work as a painter and inventor, Leonardo was also a composer and a poet, and he designed several new musical instruments, including the viola organista—which is sort of like a piano, but which bows the strings like a violin! Leonardo once wrote that music, unlike painting, disappears over time. It exists in its pure state only once, at the moment of its creation, and then suffers decay with every new performance thereafter. Now, while Leonardo was fascinated by the nature of sound waves, he didn't anticipate the invention of microphones and recording machines. But he might argue that even a recording is like the ghost of a live performance, preserving the sounds of a performance, but not the feeling of shared experience, a wonder which exists only once... like in a dream!

Have you ever dreamed of flying? What would it be like? Where would you go? How high? What sort of things might you see while you were up in the air? You could try writing a poem or a story of your experiences while flying. What kind of music would you want to hear while you were up there?

TIMELINE OF LEONARDO'S LIFE

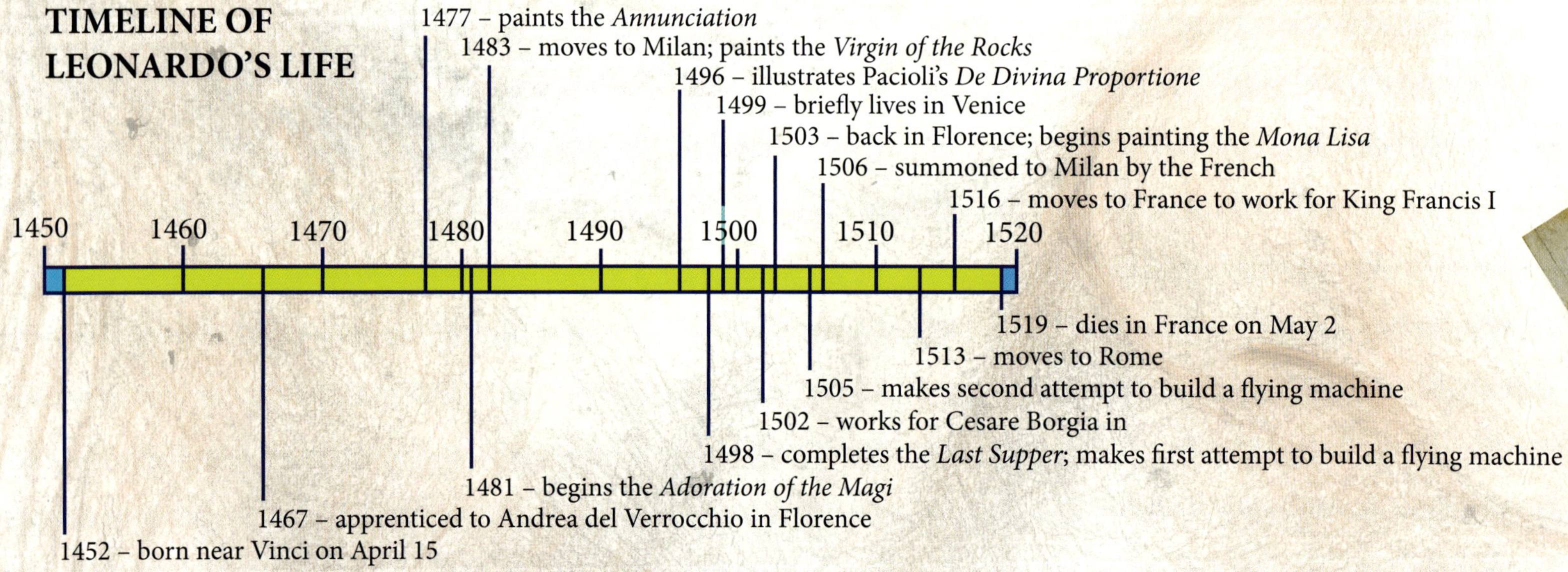

INSPIRATION

Most of the illustrations for *Leonardo Dreams of His Flying Machine* are inspired directly by specific pieces of art created by Leonardo da Vinci. Although the master left us only fifteen completed oil paintings, there are frescoes, unfinished paintings, studies, and drawings that survive that were used as direct inspiration for the illustrations in this book, taking landscape elements from one work, and figures from another, and combining them in new ways. For example, the second illustration of the book, which accompanies the first line of the poem, "Tormented by visions of flight and falling", is based on Leonardo's *Storm in an Alpine Valley* and *The Virgin and Child with Saint Anne and Saint John the Baptist*. You can almost see half a face in da Vinci's red chalk drawing. The other half reflects the ghostlike dark feeling of the underpainting for the Madonna. The merging of the two ideas illustrates the torment in the poetic line.

Storm in an AlpineValley - c.1508-10

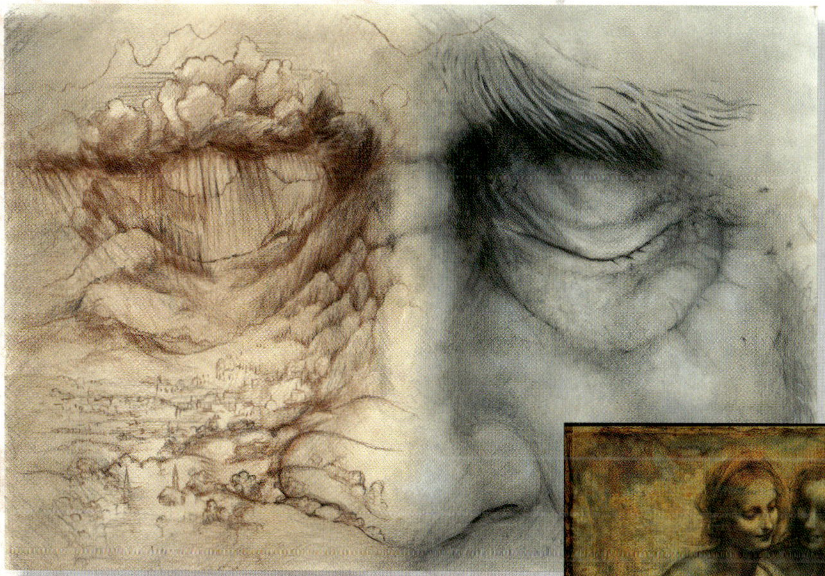

"Tormented by visions of flight and falling"

The Virgin and Child with Saint Anne and Saint John the Baptist c. 1499–1500 or c. 1506–1508

Portrait of a Musician - 1485

"As the candles burn"

Map Of Imola - 1502

"More wondrous and terrible each than the last" is the third painting. This illustration is mainly based on da Vinci's *Adoration of the Magi.* A crowd gathers with the Three Wise Men, around the Virgin Mary and her child. What a different kind of miracle it would have been if Leonardo would have figured out how to fly! The crowd is copied directly from this painting, except for the crashing pilot which was originally a pen and ink drawing. Instead of worshipping, the Magi now have scissors, tools and fabric and are builders of machines that can fly. In the illustrations here, da Vinci's sketches of flying machines are portrayed without adaptations.

"Sketch of a Helicopter" - 1493

Adoration of the Magi - 1481

"Studies for the Heads of Two Soldiers in the *Battle of Anghiari*" - 1504-05

"Sketch of a Parachute" -c. 1483

"More wondrous and terrible each than the last"

"… into the sun"

Virgin of the Rocks - 1483–1486

Annunciation - 1472-1475

The illustration for "… into the sun" is based on the *Virgin of the Rocks*, of which there are two versions. One hangs in Paris and the other in London. The town is inspired by the *Annunciation*, one of da Vinci's earlier works.

Leonardo was fascinated by birds, and the dream of flying. But he had many other interests as well. During his life he filled many notebooks covering all manner of topics, including mathematics, anatomy, zoology, physics, weaponry, music, engineering, and, of course, aeronautics. To keep the contents of these books secret, he wrote them in a special backward script that could only be read in a mirror. The notebooks in which he explored his dreams of flight include many drawings of birds and bats, detailed studies of wings, explanations of aeronautical principles, and designs for several types of flying machine. These designs have continued to fuel the imagination of dreamers and tinkerers down to the present day. You don't have to go to a museum to see Leonardo's notebooks, although doing so is a wonderful experience! Most of his notebooks have been carefully photographed and are available to explore online, including those concerning aeronautics and flying machines: the Codex Atlanticus, the Paris Manuscripts, and the Codex on the Flight of Birds. See if you can find other machines Leonardo invented.

PREPARING A PANEL

Artists can paint on many different types of surfaces. During the Renaissance, painters commonly used wooden panels as the preferred surface for their masterworks. Painters had to take many steps to prepare a panel to receive paint. First, they found a sturdy plank of hardwood, such as oak, walnut, or poplar. This board had to be cut and joined, planed, and sanded to get it ready for the next step. They sealed the surface of the wood using a glue made from animal hides, most commonly rabbit skins. Into this layer of glue they then applied a piece of linen cloth stretched across the surface of the panel, to act as a strengthening layer. Then, layer after layer of a special chalk and glue mixture called gesso was applied, each time brushed on in alternating directions, and sanded carefully before each new layer. After about ten such layers, the final sanding created a smooth, shiny surface that looked and felt like ivory, and was the perfect surface to absorb and bind to paint. If Leonardo were alive today, do you think he would make his own panels, or purchase the ready-made ones from the art store or online?

Here is how you can make a simple, inexpensive panel

These are the materials you need:

- A small piece of ¼" thick birch plywood with no knots or other imperfections
- A soft brush or paint roller for trim and doors
- Gesso from the art store
- Fine grit sandpaper on a sandblock

This is what you do:

1. With the roller or brush, cover the panel with gesso.
2. Wait until it's completely dry.
3. Sand it lightly.
4. Give it one or two more coats of gesso, repeating steps 1-3 above, but rolling on the gesso in alternate directions.
5. Sand the surface as smooth as possible without exposing the wood.

Optional: If you want to make a larger panel you might have to brace it on the back to prevent it from warping. You can also follow the example of many Renaissance painters and add some color to the gesso before applying it. This way you will not work on a stark white surface. If you want to do this, simply stir some acrylic or water-based paint into the gesso.

UNDER-PAINTING

Before Leonardo began a painting, he first drew on the surface of the gesso panel. This is the preliminary sketch of the composition. Nowadays most people draw using a pencil, which is made of soft graphite surrounded by wood; but during the Renaissance, pencils as we know them were not invented yet. Artists would often draw with a feather quill and ink; with chalk; or with a piece of charcoal, usually made from a willow branch. While these were common drawing materials during Leonardo's time, some artists would also draw on the gesso using a technique called metalpoint, which uses a pen tipped with any kind of soft metal, usually tin, lead, or silver. As you draw with the metal point, you create an image by leaving behind a tiny residue of metal-oxide, like a trail, which turns darker over time. Silver has always been the preferred metal; it is soft, not very expensive, and drawings made with it tarnish to a very attractive grey/brown on the gessoed surface.

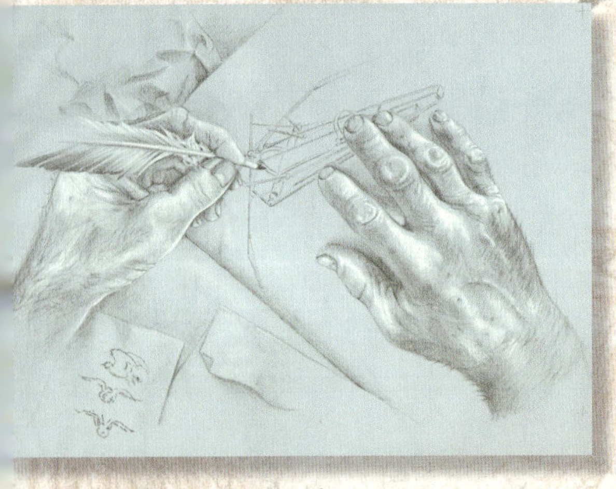

How to make a metal point drawing

These are the materials you need:

- A pencil, or a dowel or stick the size of a pencil
- Tape
- A metal wire of any kind
- Wire cutters
- Gesso or a regular wall paint in a very light color
- A brush or roller
- A white pencil (optional)
- Heavy paper
- Fine grit sandpaper

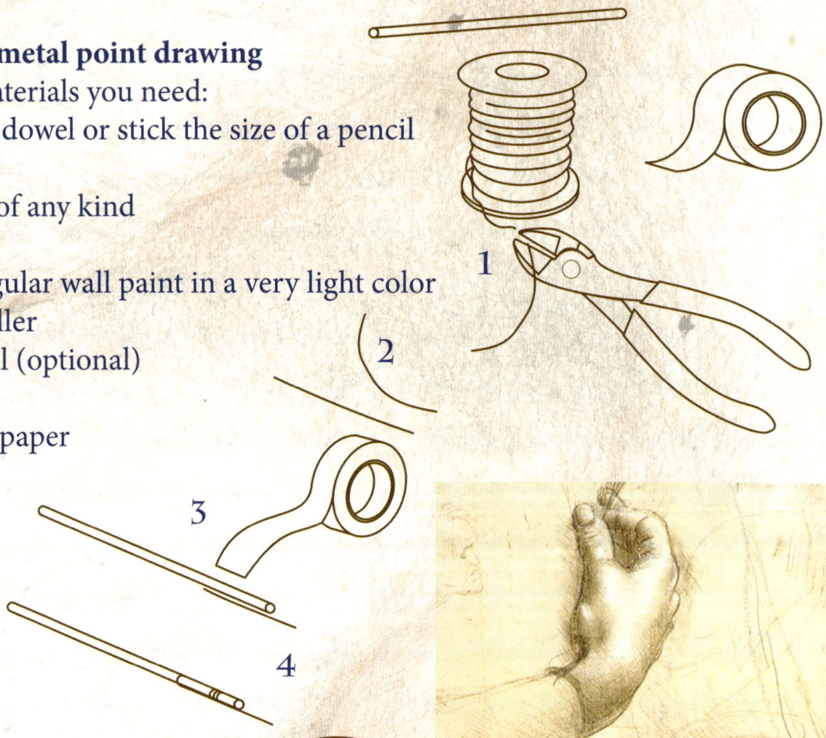

This is what you do:

1. Cut off about 4 inches of wire.
2. Bend the wire straight.
3. Tape the wire securely to the pencil or dowel, making sure that about an inch of the wire is sticking out.
4. Cover the paper with paint or gesso and let it dry.
5. Sand the gesso smooth with the sandpaper.
6. Gently draw on the paper without damaging the surface.

The paint or gesso's binder is abrasive and will sand off a little of the metal stylus and the metal residue will leave a mark on the paper. To make a line darker you will have to go over the same lines again and again until the desired tone is achieved. Copper wire will tarnish green, while silver tarnishes grey/brown; gold or steel wire create different effects, and so were only rarely used for metalpoint work.

If the paper is tinted, try to highlight some of your art with a white pencil. It will make the art seem more three dimensional.

"Study of Female Hands" - 1474

How to make an ink pen from a feather

These are the materials you need:

- A long feather about 12" with a ¼ inch diameter tube (Goose or Turkey)
- A craft knife
- Ink
- Cutting board
- Tweezers
- Paper

This is what you do:

1. Hold the feather in your hand comfortably like holding a pen and determine which side goes up. The quill end should point down to the writing surface.
2. Shave away the fuzz on the bottom and even some of the barbs, with the craft knife so you can hold the feather more like a pen.
3. Place the quill on a cutting board and cut the end at a 45-degree angle leaving the writing point on the longest side of the quill.
4. With a marker make a dot above where you would like the writing point to be.
5. Inspect the tube and remove any membranes with the tweezers.
6. Gently score the center of the opening at the bottom of the quill tube until you create a slit.
7. Dip the tip in the ink, and after you try to write with it you can reshape the tip more with the craft knife if nessesary. Think of it as the tip of a fountain pen. The better the shape, the less messy the writing.

Optional: before you turn the quill into a pen, fill an empty tin can with sand and heat it up in a 350 °F oven for 20 minutes. Remove the can and stick the end of the feather as far as possible in the hot sand. Leave until the sand is cool.
The quill will harden and shrink. After the pen is done you can dip the other end of the feather in the ink. Let it dry and it will create an attractive colored or black tip.

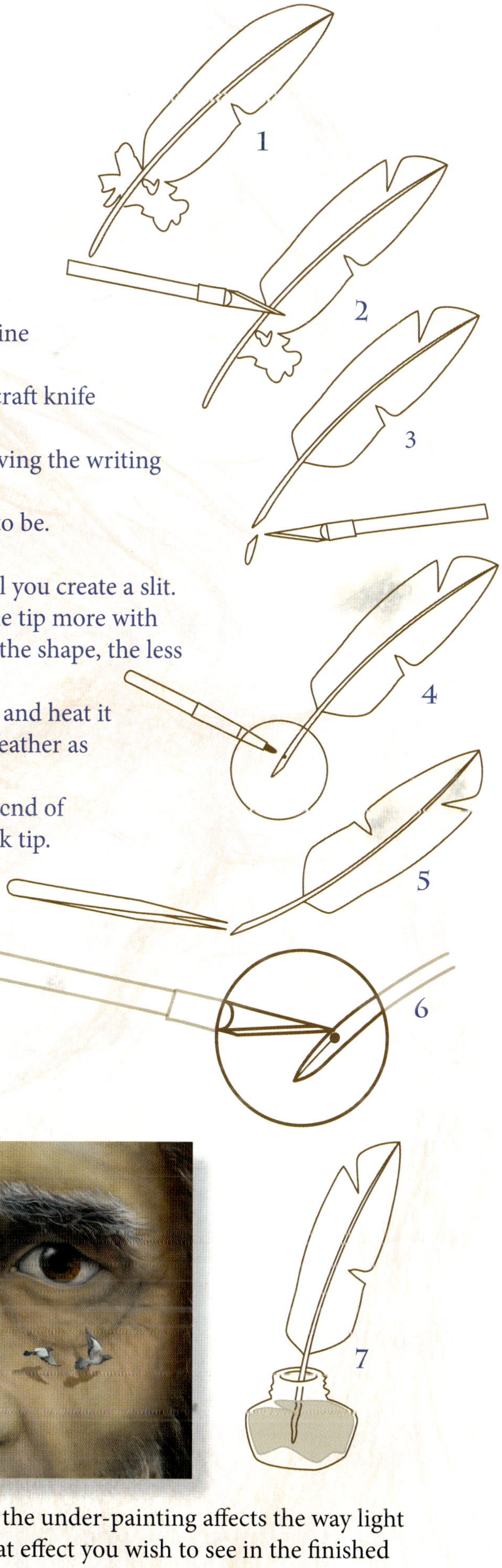

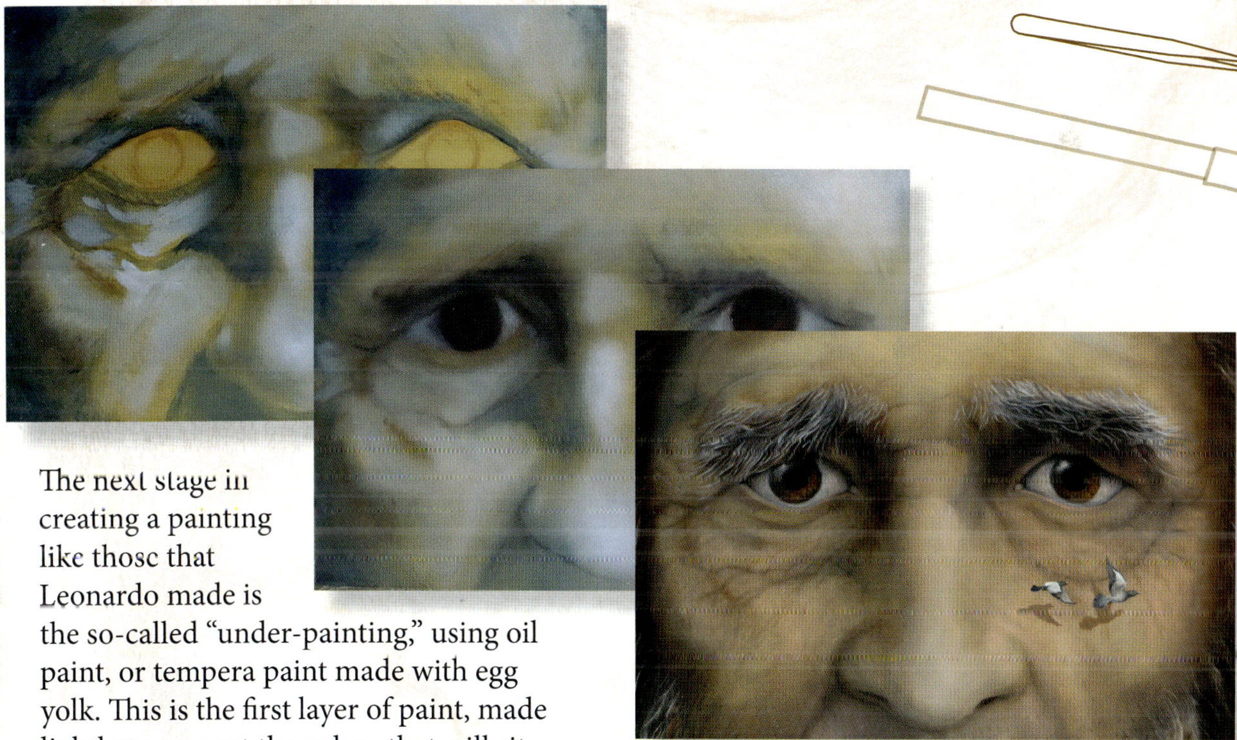

The next stage in creating a painting like those that Leonardo made is the so-called "under-painting," using oil paint, or tempera paint made with egg yolk. This is the first layer of paint, made lightly to suggest the colors that will sit on top, or in the case of skin, to create the base color. The choice of colors for the under-painting affects the way light bounces off the particles in the pigments on the surface. You must decide what effect you wish to see in the finished painting and choose an under-painting scheme to match your plan. For example, when painting a face, Renaissance painters would start the underpainting in a different color than the final skin-color, often a dark greenish-brown color called *verdaccio*. Because oil-paint is translucent, the colors underneath always have an effect on the finished work. This made it possible to paint a very realistic portrait. With each new layer, a little more oil is added to the paint to improve its flow and elasticity. This also makes the paint more transparent, which makes it possible to create shadows, to slightly change a color, or to make the color more intense. This is known as *sfumato*, which means 'smokey,' and Leonardo was a master in this technique.

PIGMENTS AND BINDERS

Since the most ancient times all paint has been made of the same basic ingredients. Different colors are produced from various types of earth, minerals, semi-precious stones, plants, and even some animal materials. These substances are ground down to a fine powder and mixed with some sort of binding material to make paint. Common natural binders in Leonardo's time included beeswax, egg yolk, oil, and a tree sap called gum arabic. Leonardo experimented with different binders on different surfaces, but most often he used layers of paint made from egg yolk, and from linseed or another kind of oil. All of the paintings in this book used paint made from pigments and walnut oil (because linseed oil tends to turn yellowish over time). During the Renaissance artists would often leave the layers of paint to dry before adding a new layer. It takes a week or more for one layer to dry and add a new one. An oil painting is only fully dry after 6 to 12 months!

Before modern resources like plastics and nylon, artists had to use all natural materials, such as wood, other plant materials, and even substances that come from animals. Here is a list:

- Animal bones and hides were used to make glue, and mixed with animal bone ashes to make gesso.
- Bones and leather were also used for mechanisms and bellows, instruments (such as in for example pipe organs), and tools.
- Ivory was used for the white piano keys, but also for decoration, and as a surface for miniature paintings.
- Different kinds of animal hair were used to make artist brushes: hog bristles for stiff brushes, and mink for soft ones. Feathers were used to make pens and fine brushes, and the quills of meat-eating birds like crows were used in the plucking mechanisms of harpsichords. Horse hair was and is still used for the bow of a violin, and the guts from sheep, goats, cattle, horses, and hogs were used for the strings.
- Shellac—a very common wood finish used for musical instruments—is made from the lac bug. The finish of a musical instrument has a huge influence on the sound, and instrument-makers still prefer it. Before the invention of vinyl, shellac was used to make phonograph records, and is considered a natural form of plastic!

Lac Bug

How to make a paint brush from a feather

Artists' brushes during the Renaissance were made of all natural materials, such as animal hairs, bristles, or feathers. An artist would need brushes of several sizes and materials, and might use up several brushes to complete a single work. Boar bristle brushes are commonly used for oil painting. Tempera artists of the Renaissance used brushes made from the tail-hairs of squirrels or minks. A feather can be used to make a very delicate brush for fine detailed work, for example when painting a face, or tiny buildings in a landscape.

These are the materials you need:

- A large feather
- A bamboo skewer
- A pair of scissors
- Paint
- Paper

This is what you do:

1. Cut the top of the feather half way in with a pair of scissors to create a point
2. Cut off the top
3. Cut off the very lower end of the quill to create a tube, and make sure the tube is open on both sides.
4. Slide the tube up on the piece you cut in step 1; it will gather the barbs together in a tiny brush with a very fine tip.
5. Insert the skewer into the other side of the tube.

Of course, with any kind of art it takes practice and a lot of experimenting to get it just right.

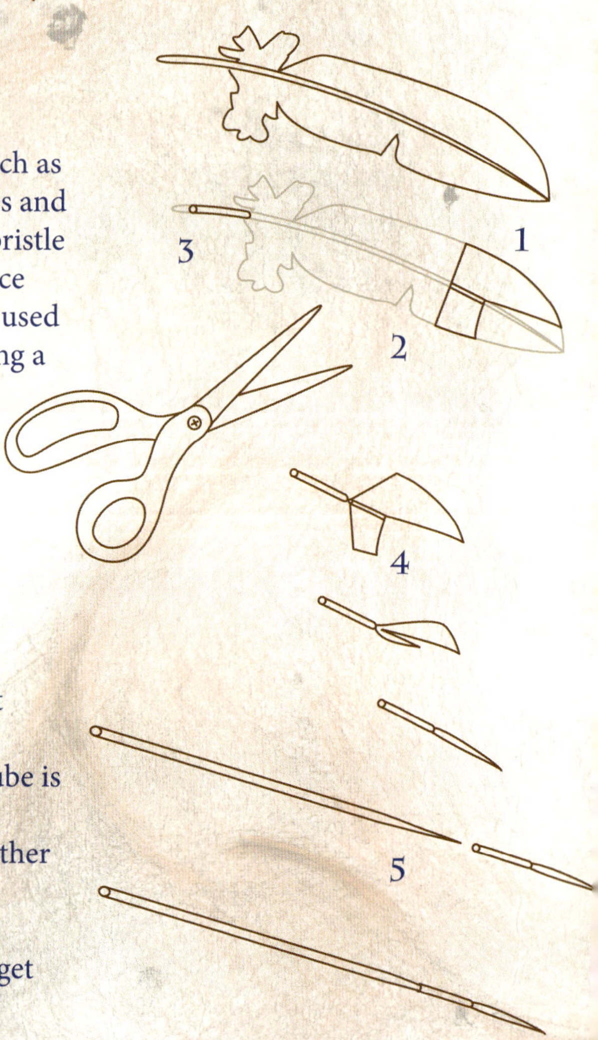

COMPOSITION

All the illustrations for this book have Leonardo's sleeping face embedded in them. In this way the idea that Leonardo is dreaming is illustrated throughout the book. For example, the ropes that hold down the Montgolfier balloon follow the outline of his nose, and the clouds are the bags under his eyes. The hands that draw the flying machine cover the eyes and the fold in the paper follows part of his nose. If you look for it you will see it in each illustration. By sharing this one unifying theme of composition, the images morph into one another as the reader turns the pages. Leonardo's dream becomes the foundation of each image, as if his spirit were overseeing what happened in the future of the history of flight.

Another important and often hidden aspect of a painting's composition is the mathematical proportions the artist uses to put the elements of the painting in just the right place. This concept of perfect mathematical proportion was very important to artists during the Renaissance. The word "Renaissance" means rebirth, and it refers to the rediscovering of the ancient Classical period in Europe, especially the ancient Greek culture. The beautiful Greek statues, architecture, and decorations were based on the principles of the Golden Ratio (also known as the Golden Section, Golden Mean, Divine Proportion, or simply by the Greek letter *phi* Φ). The Greeks believed that applying this ratio would create something visually pleasing and proportionally correct. Leonardo was known to use this principle in his art. His version of the *Vitruvian Man* is a great example. Simply said, the ratio is 1:1.618. Another famous Leonardo, Leonardo Fibonacci, wrote in 1202 CE that this ratio is found everywhere in nature; and we see it still today in everyday things like the proportions of a credit card, a logo design, or a bottle of wine, which are also designed using the Golden Ratio. If the short side measures 1, the long side should measure 1.618; or if the neck measures 1 the body of the bottle should measure 1.618.

Vitruvian Man - c.1490

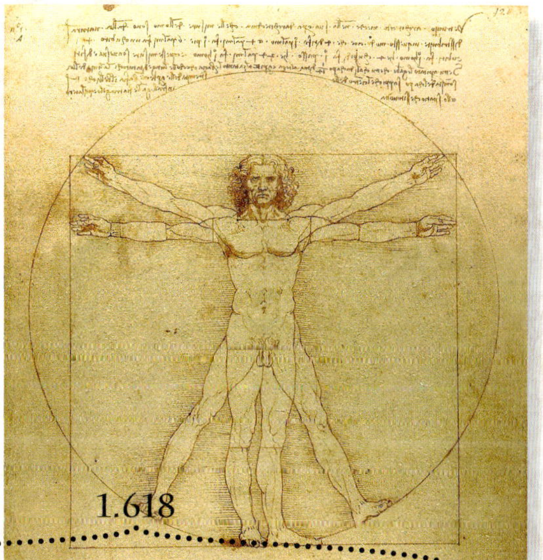

Dragon Striking down Lion

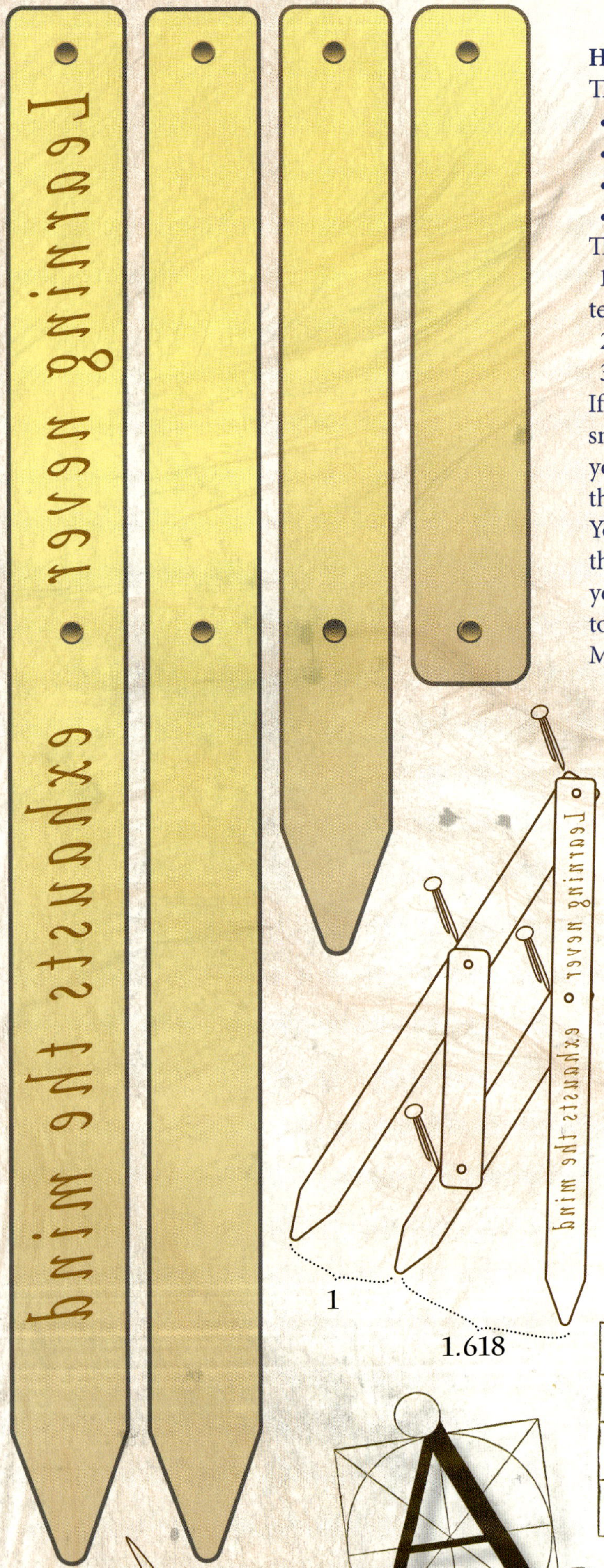

How to make a Golden Mean Caliper

These are the materials you need:

- The template to the left on this page, copied on card-stock
- A pair of scissors
- A hole punch
- 4 paper fasteners

This is what you do:

1. Cut out the parts that you need from the copy you made of the template of this page.
2. Punch holes where the parts are marked with a dot.
3. Insert the fasteners as shown in the illustration.

If you measure from your finger-tip to the first knuckle with the smaller side, the other side of the caliber should automatically give you the distance from the same knuckle to where the finger meets the palm.

You can do the same with a credit card. Measure the short side with the small opening and the large opening should automatically give you the measurement of the long side. Try it on all sorts of things to see how they are designed more or less according to the Golden Mean!

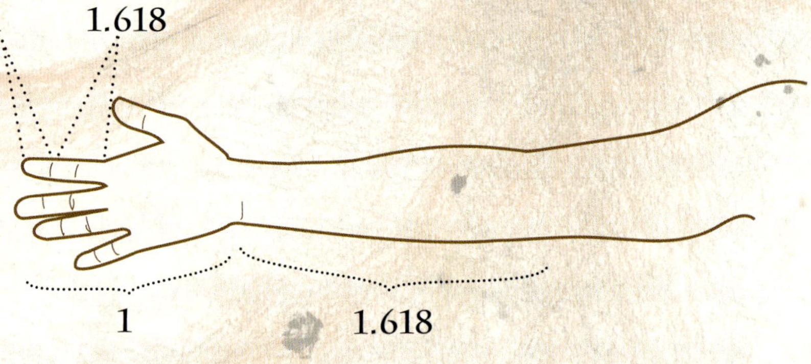

Leonardo's math teacher, Luca Pacioli, wrote *De Divina Proportione (On The Divine Proportions)* in 1496. The book was mainly about the Golden Ratio and how it could be used in architecture and design. Leonardo da Vinci made many illustrations for the book and Pacioli designed a font using the rules of the Golden Ratio.

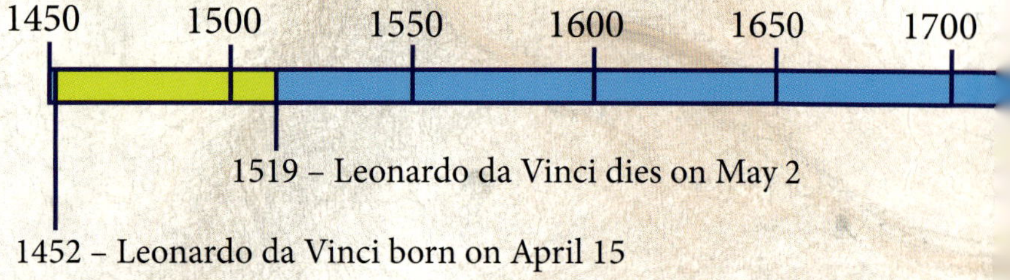

FLIGHT

Some might think that because his amazing map of the town of Imola was drawn from a bird's-eye perspective, Leonardo really *was* able to fly. The truth is that he only dreamed of flying, and created his amazing flying machines only in his imagination; but the experience and the mental wealth he gained from the process must have been incredible. Then he simply had to pass on the torch to other dreamers, who took inspiration from Leonardo's imagination and turned it into actual flight!

The first documented flight was almost 300 years after Leonardo's time, accomplished by the Montgolfier brothers in their famous hot air balloon. Their first successful attempt was in 1783, with a duck, a rooster, and a sheep in the balloon's basket! Étienne Montgolfier was the first human to go up. Their balloon was blue and gold, decorated with the *fleur-de-lis*, which was the heraldic symbol of the French monarchy, and with the face of king Louis XVl.

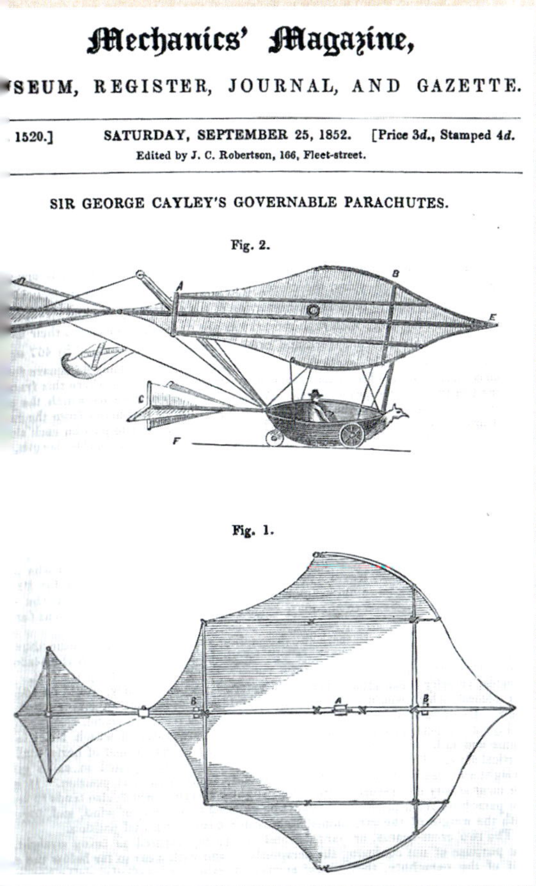
Mechanics' Magazine,

SEUM, REGISTER, JOURNAL, AND GAZETTE.

1520.] SATURDAY, SEPTEMBER 25, 1852. [Price 3d., Stamped 4d.

Edited by J. C. Robertson, 166, Fleet-street.

SIR GEORGE CAYLEY'S GOVERNABLE PARACHUTES.

Fig. 2.

Fig. 1.

Sir George Cayley's glider

The next successful attempts were a glider flown by Sir George Cayley in 1804, and the historic Wright brothers' flight a century later in 1904. Since then airplanes have gotten bigger, more powerful, and more sophisticated, able to carry people high into the atmosphere to cover distances in a few hours that once took months to traverse. And in the century since the Wright brothers' flight we have ventured even further—we have explored the moon, our solar system, and sent spacecraft hurtling into the vastness of interstellar space. Just think how far we could go, all beginning with the imagination of a dreamer like Leonardo!

Montgolfier brothers' hot air balloon

Wright brothers' powered flying machine

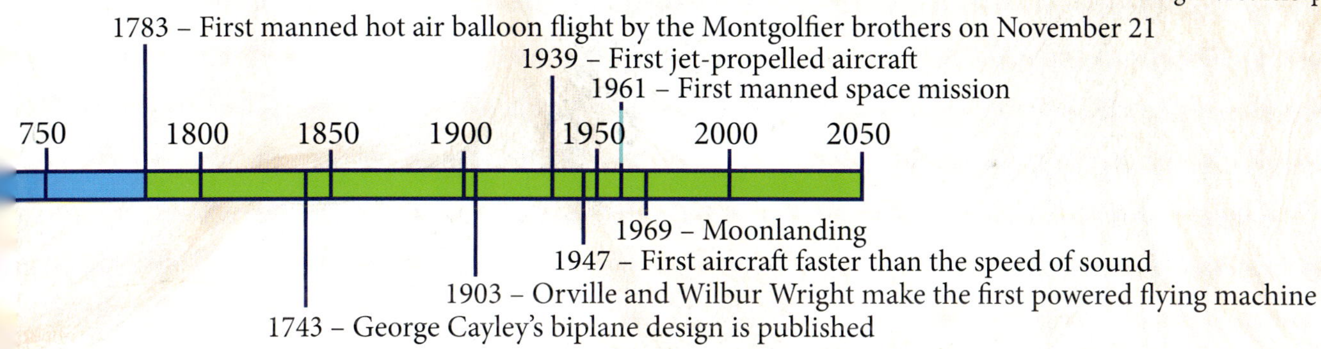

Thank you to our generous supporters! Below is a list of our Kickstarters in alphapetical order.

Neil Aaronson   Afsaneh Aayani   Susan Aber   Christopher Alexander   Jennifer Allen   The Altus/Jost Family
Tennessee & Alve Shelton   Amanda   Deri Ament   Alan Anderson   Rosanna Andrews   Catherine L Ankenbrandt   Anonymous
Molly, Bill & Liam Arbogast   Mary Ann Armstrong   L M Attea   Susan Attea   Deb & Dennis Aulich   Gabe Baker   Linda Baker
Shana C Baker   Rob Baldwin   The Baldwin Family   Treasa Bane   W Quinconnor Baron   Raberta "Boots" Barrix   Kim Bates
Robin Baysinger & Dan Siegfried   Paul & Arline Beagan   Steven Beckett & Laura Rossiter   Debora Beckley   Charlie Bencivengo
Laura Nicolle Benitez   Gregory Bennett   Volker Bernhart   Candance Bise   Betsy Bitter   Cathy Bleser   Scott Martin Brackey
Kit Bridges   Mary L Brock   Penna M Broman   Christopher Stewart Brown   Randy & Theresa Brown   Patricia Bullard   Katie Burk
Maggie Burk   John Burns   Pam Burns- in honor of all my dreamers   Claire Burrell-McDonald   Dr Kerry Burtis   Connie & Bill Burton
Wolfgang & Susan Calnin   Ethan Carlson   Mary Ongjoco Chapman   Bev Choutka   Bruce Clawson   Roberta Condon
Carol Condron   Christin Conrow   Liz Cullers   Marie D Cummings   Geri Ceci Cupery   Marjorie Cutting   Carolyn K Davis
Angel Jennifer Rosebud Dawson   Howard B Dawson   Leif A Dawson   Marti C Dawson   Valkyrie A Dawson   Bob & Becky Demaree
Henry Derr & Nia Van Laarhoven   Karen DeSanto   Sue Dietsch   Monique van Dijk   Kaya & Braya Doering   Judith Drotar
Juanita Edington   Eric Entken   Nijole Etzwiler   Kelly Erby   Isaac & Gabriel Evans   Mary L Fancher   Neal Farley
Elaine Farrar Kondrat   Michael & Michele Feld   Thomas Flock   Dan & Addy Forrest   Holly Fortier   Charlie & Max Fortney
Donald & Diana Fox   Jason E Frederick   Christopher Friesen   The Joe & Marianne Finlinson Family   Fritsch Family Dreamers
LaNelle Froehlich   Jeannie Galvin   Debbie Carley Gerencser   Emily Garlock   Jacob Garrett   Carrie Gaston   Kerrin M Gates
Tristan Gavin   Ava Marie Gehri   Ruth Getsinger   Becky & Mike Van Gheem   Miguel Gonzalez-Abellas   Keli Rena Goodchild
Bram De Graaf   Charlie & Sandy Grames   James R Green   Robert Greenham   Laurie & Leo Grill   Nathaniel Grill
Wendi Sue Grover   J Douglas Guy   Angie Haller   Jen Hagar   The Hagen Family   Aiden Michael Hale   Colette Halliday
Angela Hanley   Rylee May Harig   Theo William Harig   Connie Harrison   Darren Hart   Patrick & Kate Hart   Emily Hastreiter
Bill Hatcher & Darlene Lawrence   Julie Henze   Aria, Cora & Noelle Hiel   Wanetta Hill   Kathryn Hoelter   Monica Holden
Meyer Holmes   Steven C Holovach   André Horjus   Emma M Horjus Oliver Horjus   Sjoukje Horjus-Procee   Kathy Houzner
In honor of Rainier Jacobs Howey   Scott R Hummel   Samuel Hunter Chris Hurd   J Hutton   Mark & Lisa Ingles   Scott Ireland
Rich & Joan Jacobson   Anne De Jong-Procee   Taylor Isenring   Cristina & Lorraine De La Isla   Erin Janssen
Dallas Johnson & Karolyn Straub   Theresa Johnson   Sarah Joncas   Patrick Jones & Tom Neal   Aart & Renee de Jong   Orion Jordan
Mekai, Caleb & Jane Jordan   John Jorgensen & Olga Pomolova   Benjamin R Joseph   Alexandria Jozefowicz   Hadley S Kalish
Mayme Keagy   Garrett Keith   Loydene Keith   Julie Keller   Sarah Kidd   Julie Kingsbury   Lory Y Kitamura   Doug Klapper
Dominic R Knopp   Rachel Knott   Tom & Holly Kobza   Stuart Koehler   Greta Koenig   George & Polly Koepp
Jacob, Juliana & Jace Koepp   Mike & Karin Jo Kohlman   The Kopitzke Family   Anthony Koss   Gaile Krause   Dan Krunnfusz
Annette Kuhlmann   Susan LaBarr   Charles R LaCombe Jr   Kathleen LaCombe   Bernie & Tammy Lager   Annemie Lamon
Steven Lampinen   Kerry K Lane   Greg & Tina Lang   Jeff & Beth Lang   The Lappin Family   Doug & Margie Lawrence
Camille Lee   Ellen Lee   Jesse L Leichsenring   Marie Lemenu   Pickleball Librarian   Christopher Loeffler   Teagan Londo
Lauren Love   Tom Lovell   Reno & Julie Lovison   Tara Lucci   Teena Lyle   Brenda Lynch   D Lyons & J Wright - Future Authors
Kecia Maciel   Lora Madonia   Christopher John Maestas   Karen Mahinski   Josephine Cecilia Malleck   Richard Manthe & Steve Ramsey
Deidre Martinko   Shannon McCall   Caitlin McCall-Baron   Susan McCuistionKate McLauchlin   Baby McPhearson   Adrian Mendoza
Colleen Mendoza   Carley & Jose Mercado & Family   Amber Meyer   Marlene Meyer   Alexander Michaelson   Evelyn & Matilda Mjelde
Matt & Kappy Morin   Pierre & Shelley Mordini   Kim Morse   Colleen M Murphy   Barbara Murray   Patricia Murray
Pete Mutschler   Christen Napier   Kelly Nash   Jay Nemeth   Lance Edward Newman   Kip Nieuwenhuis   Terry & Carol Nimmer
The Nimmer & Thomas Grands   Sara Noll   James O'Donnell   Michelle Oesterle   Rebecca & Peter Oettinger   Mary Kay Olson
Rachel M Ost   The Paget Family   Atlas Parchem   Aunt Pat & Uncle Lou   Thierry Payon   Neil Peterson   Thomas Peterson
Genny Petrulis   Crosby Petty   Ruby Petty   David W Pierce   Pati Piper   Mary Pickering Webb   Alden & Evelyn Porzel
The Potter Family   Timothy, Jennifer, Danny, & Patrick Powell   The Mike & Holly Powers Family   Tom Prasch   Jan Price
Rachel Puralewski   Jim Puralewski   Leander & Livius Rajan   Faith Raiguel & Billy Weber   Tricia Rasmussen   Ria Raven
Carol & Mark Reasa   Dalton Rosenquist Reiman   Daniel Floyd Reeves   Juliette B Reiss   Tyson V Repke   Tracy Resseguie
Suzy Rhinestone   Rachel Lynn Robison   Rosanne & Dave Ricci   Raymond Charles Richter   Andrew & Brooke Robinson
Britiany Robinson   Tom Robson   Sue M Roessler   Gretchen Roltgen   Joan & Paul Romiti   Maja Roodveldt   Remco Roovers
Evan & Mallory Rossiter & Family   Jeff Roy   Clay & Shelly Sabourin   Hans Schaal   The Schick Family   Terri Schider
Donald Schlising   Amanda, Matt & Eli Schluntz   Calder Schmidt   James L Schneider   Sarah Schwartz   Allison J Scott
Marc Seals & Vivian Miller   In Loving Memory of Donna Segschneider   Don Seitz   Annika Kari Shallberg   Elzada Shaw
Holly Shaw   Terry Shelton   Lauren Sheridan   Frank Shopen   Peter & Kim Shrake   Henry & Diane Silvestri
Thomas & Emma Silvestri   Vinnie Silvestri   Patricia Skaja   The Rob Smit Family   Elisabeth Maria Smith   Kristin Smith
Spud Smith   Logan Smouter   Jason Sneegas   Ruth Anne Sneegas   Jason Sorci   Pam Sorci   Carolyn Soucy   Rebekah Sprott
Susie Sprouse   Donna Sprowles   Harm Sterenberg   Maeve Sullivan   Stephen & Karen Swallen   John & Donna Taapken
Barry & Judi Temple   Mark A Teslik   J Tidwell   Timothy Tharaldson   Roly Theule   Kimm Tomala   Cameron S Tomko
Olivia D Tomko   William S Tomko   Elizabeth & Rob Toms   Peter & Lisinka de Vries-Schuring   Paco Valera
Ben Varnum & Megan Griffiths   Sophia Lopez Velarde   Gretchen Viney   Ann & Jeff Vogtschaller   The Vrabec Family
The Vriesacker Family   JoEllen Waddell   Jessica Wagner   The Walechka Family   Ulf Wallentin   Libby Weber   Sandy Weber
Beth Weisman   Tracy Weisman   Lauren Welch   West Aurora Madrigal Singers   Gregory & Grace Weston   Wild Bird Barn
Bram Williams   Sean Williams   The Wilson Family   Addison Winecke   Bruce Witte MD   Cecilia & William Wolfe
Ernie & Rita Wittwer   Keith Woodson   Kasch Ziehmke   Jane Zimmerman   Michael Zolper